AIR FRYER COOKBOOK FOR BEGINNERS

by Luke Grzesica

© Copyright 2024 Luke Grzesica
All rights reserved.
No part of the contents of this book may be reproduced, duplicated by electronic or mechanical means transmitted without the direct written permission of the author or publisher.
In no event shall the publisher or the author be held legally responsible for any damage, compensation or monetary loss caused directly or indirectly by the information contained in this book.
Legal Notice:
This book is copyrighted and is intended for personal use only. You may not alter, distribute, sell, use, quote or paraphrase any part or content of this book without the author's permission.
Disclaimer Note:
Please note that the information contained in this document is for educational and entertainment purposes.
The content of this book is derived from various sources and the author's knowledge of the subject matter. Every effort has been made to present accurate, up-to-date, reliable and complete information.
No guarantees are declared or implied. Readers acknowledge that the author does not provide legal, financial, medical or professional advice. A licensed professional should be consulted before attempting any of the techniques presented in this book.
By reading this document, the reader accepts that the author is not liable for any damages, direct or indirect, incurred as a result of the use of the information contained in this document, including, but not limited to, inaccuracies.

INTRODUCTION

Welcome to the exciting world of cooking with an air fryer! Our kitchens are evolving, and innovative appliances like air fryers are opening up new possibilities for preparing healthy and delicious meals. With this technology, you can enjoy crispy, juicy, and flavorful dishes using minimal oil, making meals healthier and less calorie-dense. This book is designed to help you unlock the full potential of this versatile appliance and learn how to prepare delectable dishes quickly and easily.

In this book, you will find a collection of recipes tailored to the tastes and preferences of the UK audience. From classic dishes like fish and chips to modern, healthy options, the air fryer allows you to create mouthwatering meals in just a few minutes.

We will start with the basics: we will discuss different models of air fryers, their functions, and how to use them to achieve the best results. We will also share some practical tips on maintenance and cleaning to ensure your appliance serves you for years to come.

I invite you on a culinary journey full of inspiration and flavors. Whether you are an experienced chef or a beginner in the world of air fryers, you will find recipes that will surprise you with their simplicity and efficiency. Discover how easy and enjoyable it is to cook healthy and tasty dishes with an air fryer!

How to Use an Air Fryer: Basic Tips and Safety

An air fryer is an appliance that uses hot air to fry and bake foods, achieving results similar to deep frying but with minimal oil. This allows you to enjoy healthier and less calorie-dense meals. To make the most of your air fryer, follow these tips :

1. Preparation:
Ensure the air fryer is placed on a stable, flat surface.
Wash all removable parts, such as the basket and tray, before first use.
Dry them thoroughly before reassembling.

2. Cooking:
Preheat the air fryer according to the recipe you want to follow.
This often requires turning on the appliance a few minutes before adding the food.
Make sure the foods are thawed and dry for the best results.
Depending on the recipe, you can spray or brush the foods with a small amount of oil to enhance crispiness.
Arrange the foods in the basket evenly, ensuring they do not overlap, to allow for even cooking.
Cook the foods according to the recipe instructions, adjusting the temperature and time to your specific appliance.

3. Cooking Monitoring and Safety:
Check on the foods occasionally during cooking to ensure they are not burning.
Stir or flip the foods to promote even cooking.
Never place plastic or other flammable materials in the air fryer basket.
Use oven mitts when removing the basket with hot food to avoid burns.
Avoid overloading the appliance with foods or ingredients, as this can lead to uneven cooking or potential damage.
After cooking, turn off the appliance and allow it to cool down before cleaning.

5. Cleaning and Maintenance:
Once the appliance has cooled, remove the basket and other detachable parts and wash them in warm, soapy water or in the dishwasher if possible.
Clean the interior of the appliance with a damp cloth, then dry it thoroughly.

RECIPES
APPETIZERS

RECIPE FOR AIR-FRIED ZUCCHINI CHIPS
WITH PAPRIKA FLAVOR

Short Description: Enjoy a healthy, flavorful, and crispy alternative to traditional potato chips with these air-fried zucchini chips. Lightly seasoned and quick to prepare, these chips make the perfect snack or appetizer.

Preparation Time: 15 minutes
Cooking Time: 8–10 minutes
Number of Servings: 2
Nutritional Information (per serving):

- Calories: 90 kcal
- Protein: 1.5 g
- Fat: 7 g
- Carbohydrates: 6 g
- Fiber: 1.5 g
- Sodium: 300 mg

Ingredients:
2 medium zucchini
2 tablespoons olive oil
1/2 teaspoon salt
1/2 teaspoon black pepper
1/2 teaspoon garlic powder
1/2 teaspoon smoked paprika powder
Grated Parmesan cheese

Preparation:
1. Prepare the zucchini: Wash and dry the zucchini. Slice them into thin, even chips using a mandoline slicer or a sharp knife.
2. Season the chips: Place the zucchini chips in a large bowl. Add olive oil, salt, pepper, garlic powder, and smoked paprika (if using). Toss the chips until they are evenly coated with the seasoning.
3. Preheat the air fryer: Preheat the air fryer to 180°C (350°F) for about 5 minutes.
4. Cook the chips: Arrange the seasoned zucchini chips in a single layer in the air fryer basket. Cook for 8–10 minutes, shaking the basket halfway through to ensure even cooking.
5. Check for doneness: Keep an eye on the chips and cook them until they are crispy and golden brown.
6. To serve: Once done, remove the zucchini chips from the fryer and they are ready to serve. Sprinkle paprika powder or grated Parmesan cheese on top to taste.

RECIPE FOR AIR-FRIED GARLIC MUSHROOMS WITH PARMESAN AND PEPPERS

Short Description: These air-fried garlic Parmesan mushrooms are a delicious and savory appetizer or side dish. The mushrooms are coated in a flavorful mixture of garlic and Parmesan cheese, creating a crispy and irresistible snack.

Preparation Time: 10 minutes
Cooking Time: 8–10 minutes
Number of Servings: 2
Nutritional Information (per serving):

- Calories: 150 kcal
- Protein: 6 g
- Fat: 11 g
- Carbohydrates: 6 g
- Fiber: 1 g
- Sodium: 350 mg

Ingredients:
300 g button mushrooms, cleaned and stems trimmed
2 tablespoons olive oil
2 cloves garlic, minced
1/4 teaspoon salt, paprika powder
1/4 teaspoon black pepper
1/4 cup grated Parmesan cheese
1/4 teaspoon dried thyme
Fresh parsley, chopped

Preparation:
1. Prepare the mushrooms: Clean the mushrooms and trim the stems as needed. Pat them dry with a paper towel.
2. Mix the seasoning: In a large bowl, combine olive oil, minced garlic, salt, and black pepper. Add dried thyme if desired.
3. Coat the mushrooms: Add the mushrooms to the bowl and toss them in the seasoning mixture until they are evenly coated.
4. Preheat the air fryer: Preheat the air fryer to 200°C (390°F) for about 5 minutes.
5. Cook the mushrooms: Place the seasoned mushrooms in a single layer in the air fryer basket. Cook for 8–10 minute, shaking the basket halfway through cooking to ensure even browning.
6. Add Parmesan cheese: In the last minute of cooking, sprinkle the grated Parmesan cheese over the mushrooms and continue cooking until the cheese is melted and slightly crispy.
7. Serving: Once cooked, remove the mushrooms from the fryer and sprinkle with paprika.

RECIPE FOR AIR-FRIED MOZZARELLA STICKS WITH OREGANO

Short Description: Enjoy a popular snack with these air-fried mozzarella sticks, featuring a crispy golden crust and gooey melted cheese inside. Serve them with marinara sauce for a classic appetizer.

Preparation Time: 10 minutes
Cooking Time: 6–8 minutes
Number of Servings: 2
Nutritional Information (per serving):

- Calories: 300 kcal
- Protein: 18 g
- Fat: 16 g
- Carbohydrates: 22 g
- Fiber: 1 g
- Sodium: 600 mg

Ingredients:
8 mozzarella cheese sticks
1/2 cup all-purpose flour
2 large eggs, beaten
1 cup breadcrumbs
1/2 teaspoon garlic powder
1/2 teaspoon dried Italian herbs
1/2 teaspoon dried oregano
1/4 teaspoon salt
1/4 teaspoon black pepper, Marinara sauce

Preparation:
1. Prepare the breading stations: Place the flour, beaten eggs, and breadcrumbs in separate shallow dishes.
2. Season the breadcrumbs: In the breadcrumbs, add garlic powder, dried Italian herbs, dried oregano, salt, and black pepper. Mix well to combine.
3. Coat the mozzarella sticks: Dredge each mozzarella stick in the flour, then dip in the beaten eggs, and finally coat with the seasoned breadcrumbs. Press the breadcrumbs gently to adhere to the cheese.
4. Preheat the air fryer: Preheat the air fryer to 200°C (390°F) for about 5 minutes.
5. Cook the mozzarella sticks: place them in a single layer in the fryer basket. Cook for 6-8 minutes, turning them halfway through, until golden brown and crispy.
6. To serve: Once cooked, remove the mozzarella sticks from the fryer and serve with the sauce.

RECIPE FOR AIR FRIED AVOCADO FRIES WITH MARJORAM

Short Description: Air-fried avocado fries are a healthy and delicious alternative to traditional fries. The avocado wedges are coated in a crispy breadcrumb mixture and air-fried to perfection for a creamy, flavorful appetizer.

Preparation Time: 10 minutes
Cooking Time: 8–10 minutes
Number of Servings: 2
Nutritional Information (per serving):

- Calories: 180 kcal
- Protein: 3 g
- Fat: 14 g
- Carbohydrates: 10 g
- Fiber: 5 g
- Sodium: 150 mg

Ingredients:
2 ripe avocados
1/2 cup all-purpose flour,2 large eggs, beaten
1 cup breadcrumbs,1/2 teaspoon chili powder
1/2 teaspoon garlic powder
1/4 teaspoon salt,1/4 teaspoon black pepper
Cooking spray,majoram
Fresh lime wedges ,Your favorite dipping sauce

Preparation:

1. Prepare the avocados: Cut each avocado and remove the pit.Slice each half into wedges.
2. Prepare the breading stations: Place the flour, beaten eggs, and breadcrumbs in separate shallow dishes.
3. Season the breadcrumbs: In the breadcrumbs, add chili powder, garlic powder, salt, and black pepper. Mix well to combine.
4. Coat the avocado wedges: Dredge each avocado wedge in the flour, then dip in the beaten eggs, and finally coat with the seasoned breadcrumbs. Press the breadcrumbs gently to adhere to the avocado.
5. Preheat the air fryer: Preheat the air fryer to 200°C (390°F) for about 5 minutes.
6. Cook the avocado fries: Lightly spray the avocado wedges with cooking spray and place them in a single layer in the air fryer basket. Cook for 8–10 minutes, flipping them halfway through, until golden brown and crispy.
7. Serve: Once cooked, remove the avocado fries from the air fryer and serve them immediately with fresh lime wedges and your favorite dipping sauce.

RECIPE FOR AIR-FRIED SWEET POTATO WEDGES WITH OREGANO

Short Description: Air-fried sweet potato wedges are a healthy and flavorful alternative to traditional fries. These wedges are lightly seasoned with oregano and other spices, cooked to perfection, resulting in a crispy exterior and tender interior.

Preparation Time: 10 minutes
Cooking Time: 12-15 minutes
Number of Servings: 2
Nutritional Information (per serving):

- Calories: 140 kcal
- Protein: 2 g
- Fat: 5 g
- Carbohydrates: 23 g
- Fiber: 3 g
- Sodium: 180 mg

Ingredients:
2 medium sweet potatoes
1 tablespoon olive oil
1/2 teaspoon smoked paprika
1/2 teaspoon garlic powder
1/2 teaspoon onion powder
1/2 teaspoon dried oregano
1/4 teaspoon salt, 1/4 teaspoon black pepper
Fresh parsley, chopped (for garnish, optional)

Preparation:
1. Prepare the sweet potatoes: Wash and peel the sweet potatoes if desired. Cut them into wedges of even thickness.
2. Season the wedges: In a large bowl, toss the sweet potato wedges with olive oil, smoked paprika, garlic powder, onion powder, dried oregano, salt, and black pepper until evenly coated.
3. Preheat the air fryer: Preheat the air fryer to 200°C (390°F) for about 5 minutes.
4. Cook the sweet potato wedges: Place the seasoned sweet potato wedges in a single layer in the air fryer basket. Cook for 12–15 minutes, flipping the wedges halfway through, until they are crispy on the outside and tender on the inside.
5. To serve: Once cooked, remove the sweet potato pieces from the fryer and garnish
6. with chopped fresh parsley, if desired. serve with a sprinkle of oregano.

RECIPE FOR AIR-FRIED PANKO-CRUSTED SHRIMP WITH OREGANO

Short Description: Crispy and juicy, these air-fried panko-crusted shrimp make a delightful appetizer. The panko breadcrumbs provide a satisfying crunch, while the shrimp are perfectly cooked.

Preparation Time: 10 minutes
Cooking Time: 8-10 minutes
Number of Servings: 2
Nutritional Information (per serving):

- Calories: 200 kcal
- Protein: 15 g
- Fat: 9 g
- Carbohydrates: 15 g
- Fiber: 1 g
- Sodium: 400 mg

Ingredients:
12 large shrimp, peeled and deveined
1/2 cup panko breadcrumbs
2 large eggs, beaten
1/2 cup all-purpose flour
1/2 teaspoon garlic powder
1/2 teaspoon paprika,1/4 teaspoon salt
1/4 teaspoon black pepper,oregano
Lemon wedges,opction cooking spray

Preparation:
1. Prepare the shrimp: Wash and dry the shrimp thoroughly, then season them with salt and black pepper.
2. Prepare the breading stations: In separate shallow dishes, place flour, beaten eggs, and panko breadcrumbs.
3. Season the breadcrumbs: In the panko breadcrumbs, mix in garlic powder and paprika for added flavor.
4. Coat the shrimp: Dredge each shrimp in the flour, dip in the beaten eggs, and coat with the seasoned panko breadcrumbs.
5. Preheat the air fryer: Preheat the air fryer to 200°C (390°F) for about 5 minutes.
6. Cook the shrimp: Arrange the breaded shrimp in a single layer in the air fryer basket. Cook for 8–10 minutes, flipping them halfway through, until golden brown and crispy.
7. To serve: Once cooked, remove the shrimp from the fryer and serve immediately with lemon wedges, witch oregano if desired.

RECIPE FOR AIR FRIED GREEK FETA BITES WITH MARJORAM

Short Description: Air-fried Greek feta bites are a delightful combination of creamy feta cheese and crispy phyllo pastry. These bite-sized treats are perfect for any gathering.

Preparation Time: 15minutes
Cooking Time: 8-10 minutes
Number of Servings: 2
Nutritional Information (per serving):

- Calories: 160 kcal
- Protein: 6 g
- Fat: 10 g
- Carbohydrates: 12 g
- Fiber: 1 g
- Sodium: 500 mg

Ingredients:
100 g feta cheese, crumbled
1/2 cup chopped fresh spinach
1 tablespoon chopped fresh dill
1/2 teaspoon dried oregano
1/4 teaspoon black pepper
6 sheets phyllo pastry
2 tablespoons melted butter, majoram

Preparation:
1. Prepare the filling: In a bowl, combine crumbled feta cheese, chopped fresh spinach, dill, dried oregano, and black pepper until well mixed.
2. Prepare the phyllo sheets: Cut the phyllo sheets into smaller squares and keep them covered with a damp cloth to prevent drying.
3. Assemble the bites: Place a small amount of the feta mixture in the center of each phyllo square, then fold the squares into triangles, brushing the edges with melted butter to seal.
4. Preheat the air fryer: Preheat the air fryer to 200°C (390°F) for about 5 minutes.
5. Cook the feta bites: Arrange the assembled feta bites in a single layer in the air fryer basket. Cook for 8–10 minutes until golden brown.
6. To serve: Remove the cooked feta bites from the air fryer and serve them warm, sprinkling with marjoram.

RECIPE FOR AIR-FRIED JALAPEÑO POPPERS WITH SAUCE

Short Description: Spicy jalapeño peppers are stuffed with a cheesy mixture and air-fried to perfection for a delicious and flavorful appetizer.

Preparation Time: 15 minutes
Cooking Time: 10-12 minutes
Number of Servings: 2
Nutritional Information (per serving):

- Calories: 180 kcal
- Protein: 8 g
- Fat: 12 g
- Carbohydrates: 8 g
- Fiber: 2 g
- Sodium: 380 mg

Ingredients:
6 large jalapeño peppers
100 g cream cheese
1/4 cup shredded cheddar cheese
1/4 teaspoon garlic powder
1/4 teaspoon dried oregano
1/4 teaspoon salt
1/4 teaspoon black pepper
1/4 cup panko breadcrumbs

Preparation:
1. Prepare the jalapeños: Cut the jalapeños in half lengthwise and remove seeds and membranes for a milder flavor.
2. Prepare the filling: In a bowl, combine cream cheese, shredded cheddar cheese, garlic powder, dried oregano, salt, and black pepper.
3. Stuff the jalapeños: Fill each jalapeño half with the cheese mixture, then top with panko breadcrumbs.
4. Preheat the air fryer: Preheat the air fryer to 200°C (390°F) for about 5 minutes.
5. Cook the jalapeño poppers: Arrange the stuffed jalapeños in a single layer in the air fryer basket. Cook for 10–12 minutes until the poppers are tender and golden.
6. To serve: Once cooked, remove the poppers from the fryer and serve immediately.

RECIPE FOR AIR FRIED COCONUT SHRIMP WITH OREGANO

Short Description: Air-fried coconut shrimp are crispy and flavorful, thanks to a coating of coconut and breadcrumbs. Serve with a sweet dipping sauce for a perfect appetizer.

Preparation Time: 10 minutes
Cooking Time: 8-10 minutes
Number of Servings: 2
Nutritional Information (per serving):

- Calories: 220 kcal
- Protein: 16 g
- Fat: 11 g
- Carbohydrates: 16 g
- Fiber: 1 g
- Sodium: 400 mg

Ingredients:
1/2 cup panko breadcrumbs
1/2 cup shredded coconut
2 large eggs, beaten
1/2 cup all-purpose flour
1/4 teaspoon salt
1/4 teaspoon black pepper
Oregano, Cooking spray
Sweet dipping sauce (optional)

Preparation:
1. Prepare the shrimp: Wash and dry the shrimp thoroughly, then season them with salt and black pepper.
2. Prepare the breading stations: In separate shallow dishes, place flour, beaten eggs, and a mixture of panko breadcrumbs and shredded coconut.
3. Coat the shrimp: Dredge each shrimp in the flour, dip in the beaten eggs, and coat with the coconut panko mixture.
4. Preheat the air fryer: Preheat the air fryer to 200°C (390°F) for about 5 minutes.
5. Cook the shrimp: Arrange the breaded shrimp in a single layer in the air fryer basket. Cook for 8–10 minutes until golden and crispy.
6. To serve: Once cooked, remove the shrimp from the fryer and serve with sweet sauce if desired and sprinkle with oregano.

RECIPE FOR FRIED ASPARAGUS WITH PARMESAN CHEESE AND MARJORAM

Short Description: Air-fried Parmesan asparagus is a tasty and healthy appetizer. The asparagus spears are seasoned and coated with Parmesan cheese, resulting in a delightful crunch.

Preparation Time: 10 minutes
Cooking Time: 8-10 minutes
Number of Servings: 2
Nutritional Information (per serving):

- Calories: 120 kcal
- Protein: 6 g
- Fat: 7 g
- Carbohydrates: 10 g
- Fiber: 4 g
- Sodium: 320 mg

Ingredients:
1 bunch of asparagus, trimmed
2 tablespoons olive oil
1/2 teaspoon garlic powder
1/2 teaspoon dried oregano
1/4 teaspoon salt,marjoram
1/4 teaspoon black pepper
1/4 cup grated Parmesan cheese

Preparation:
1. Prepare the asparagus: Wash and trim the ends of the asparagus.
2. Season the asparagus: In a bowl, toss the asparagus with olive oil, garlic powder, dried oregano, salt, and black pepper.
3. Preheat the air fryer: Preheat the air fryer to 200°C (390°F) for about 5 minutes.
4. Cook the asparagus: Arrange the asparagus spears in a single layer in the air fryer basket. Cook for 8–10 minutes, shaking the basket halfway through, until the asparagus is tender and slightly crispy.
5. To serve: Once cooked, remove the asparagus from the fryer and sprinkle with grated Parmesan and marjoram. Serve immediately.

RECIPES
MAIN COURSES MEAT

RECIPES FOR AIR-FRIED HONEY MUSTARD CHICKEN WINGS

Short Description: These air-fried honey mustard chicken wings are crispy, sticky, and bursting with sweet and tangy flavors. A perfect appetizer or main course for any occasion.

Preparation Time: 15 minutes
Cooking Time: 20-25 minutes
Number of Servings: 4
Nutritional Information (per serving):

- Calories: 280 kcal
- Protein: 21 g
- Fat: 18 g
- Carbohydrates: 7 g
- Fiber: 0 g
- Sodium: 560 mg

Ingredients:
500 g chicken wings, separated into drumettes and flats
1 tablespoon olive oil
1 teaspoon smoked paprika
1/2 teaspoon garlic powder
1/2 teaspoon onion powder
1/2 teaspoon salt, 1/4 cup honey
1/4 teaspoon black pepper
2 tablespoons Dijon mustard
1 tablespoon apple cider vinegar

Preparation:
1. Prepare the chicken wings: Pat dry the chicken wings and place them in a large bowl.
2. Season the wings: In a small bowl, mix olive oil, smoked paprika, garlic powder, onion powder, salt, and black pepper. Toss the chicken wings with the seasoning mixture until evenly coated.
3. Preheat the air fryer: Preheat the air fryer to 200°C (390°F) for about 5 minutes.
4. Cook the wings: Place the seasoned chicken wings in a single layer in the air fryer basket. Cook for 20 minutes, flipping halfway through, until the wings are golden brown and crispy.
5. Prepare the honey mustard sauce: In a small bowl, combine honey, Dijon mustard, and apple cider vinegar.
6. Toss the wings in the sauce: Once the wings are cooked, remove them from the air fryer and toss them in the honey mustard sauce until evenly coated.
7. To serve: Serve the honey mustard chicken wings warm.

RECIPES FOR AIR FRYER BBQ PORK CHOPS

Short Description: Succulent pork chops marinated in a smoky BBQ sauce, cooked in the air fryer for a crispy finish.

Preparation Time: 15 minutes
Cooking Time: 20-25 minutes
Number of Servings: 4
Nutritional Information (per serving):

- Calories: 310 kcal
- Protein: 26 g
- Fat: 16 g
- Carbohydrates: 10 g
- Fiber: 1 g
- Sodium: 450 mg

Ingredients:
4 boneless pork chops
1/2 cup BBQ sauce
1 tablespoon olive oil
1 teaspoon smoked paprika
Salt and pepper to taste

Preparation:
1. Prepare the pork chops: Pat dry the pork chops and place them in a large bowl.
2. Season the pork chops: In a small bowl, mix BBQ sauce, olive oil, smoked paprika, salt, and pepper. Toss the pork chops with the seasoning mixture until evenly coated.
3. Preheat the air fryer: Preheat the air fryer to 200°C (390°F) for about 5 minutes.
4. Cook the pork chops: Place the seasoned pork chops in a single layer in the air fryer basket. Cook for 20-25 minutes, flipping halfway through, until the pork chops are cooked through and crispy on the outside.
5. To serve: Serve the BBQ pork chops with your choice of side dish.

RECIPES FOR AIR FRYER CAJUN SHRIMP

Short Description: Juicy shrimp seasoned with Cajun spices, cooked in the air fryer for a quick and flavorful dish.

Preparation Time: 10 minutes
Cooking Time: 10 minutes
Number of Servings: 4
Nutritional Information (per serving):

- Calories: 180 kcal
- Protein: 25 g
- Fat: 8 g
- Carbohydrates: 2 g
- Fiber: 1 g
- Sodium: 600 mg

Ingredients:
400 g large shrimp, peeled and deveined
1 tablespoon olive oil
1 tablespoon Cajun seasoning
1/2 teaspoon garlic powder
1/2 teaspoon paprika

Preparation:
1. Prepare the shrimp: Pat dry the shrimp and place them in a large bowl.
2. Season the shrimp: In a small bowl, mix olive oil, Cajun seasoning, garlic powder, and paprika. Toss the shrimp with the seasoning mixture until evenly coated.
3. Preheat the air fryer: Preheat the air fryer to 200°C (390°F) for about 5 minutes.
4. Cook the shrimp: Place the seasoned shrimp in a single layer in the air fryer basket. Cook for 8-10 minutes, flipping halfway through, until the shrimp are cooked through.
5. To serve: Serve the Cajun shrimp with rice or a side salad.

RECIPES FOR AIR FRYER GARLIC HERB PORK TENDERLOIN

Short Description: Pork tenderloin seasoned with garlic, herbs, and lemon zest, cooked in the air fryer for a juicy and flavorful main course.

Preparation Time: 15 minutes
Cooking Time: 20-25 minutes
Number of Servings: 4
Nutritional Information (per serving):

- Calories: 300 kcal
- Protein: 28 g
- Fat: 15 g
- Carbohydrates: 5 g
- Fiber: 1 g
- Sodium: 420 mg

Ingredients:
500 g pork tenderloin
2 tablespoons olive oil
2 cloves garlic, minced
Zest of 1 lemon
1 teaspoon dried rosemary
1 teaspoon dried thyme
Salt and pepper to taste

Preparation:
1. Prepare the pork: Pat dry the pork tenderloin and place it in a large bowl.
2. Season the pork: In a small bowl, mix olive oil, garlic, lemon zest, rosemary, thyme, salt, and pepper. Rub the pork tenderloin with the seasoning mixture until evenly coated.
3. Preheat the air fryer: Preheat the air fryer to 200°C (390°F) for about 5 minutes.
4. Cook the pork: Place the seasoned pork tenderloin in the air fryer basket. Cook for 20-25 minutes, turning halfway through, until the pork is cooked through and reaches an internal temperature of 63°C (145°F).
5. To serve: Let the pork rest for 5 minutes before slicing. Serve with roasted vegetables or a salad.

RECIPES FOR AIR FRYER GREEK-STYLE LAMB CHOPS

Short Description: Juicy lamb chops marinated in Greek-style herbs and lemon juice, cooked in the air fryer for a flavorful and tender main course.

Preparation Time: 20 minutes
Cooking Time: 15 minutes
Number of Servings: 4
Nutritional Information (per serving):

- Calories: 320 kcal
- Protein: 28 g
- Fat: 20 g
- Carbohydrates: 3 g
- Fiber: 1 g
- Sodium: 370 mg

Ingredients:
4 lamb chops
2 tablespoons olive oil
Juice of 1 lemon
2 cloves garlic, minced
1 teaspoon dried oregano
1 teaspoon dried mint
Salt and pepper to taste

Preparation:
1. Prepare the lamb chops: Pat dry the lamb chops and place them in a large bowl.
2. Season the lamb chops: In a small bowl, mix olive oil, lemon juice, garlic, oregano, mint, salt, and pepper. Rub the lamb chops with the seasoning mixture until evenly coated.
3. Preheat the air fryer: Preheat the air fryer to 200°C (390°F) for about 5 minutes.
4. Cook the lamb chops: Place the seasoned lamb chops in the air fryer basket. Cook for 15 minutes, flipping halfway through, until the lamb chops reach the desired level of doneness.
5. To serve: Serve the Greek-style lamb chops with a side of couscous or a Greek salad.

RECIPES FOR AIR FRYER LEMON HERB CHICKEN THIGHS

Short Description: Flavorful chicken thighs marinated in lemon, garlic, and herbs, cooked in the air fryer for a delicious and juicy meal.

Preparation Time: 15 minutes
Cooking Time: 20-25 minutes
Number of Servings: 4
Nutritional Information (per serving):

- Calories: 290 kcal
- Protein: 25 g
- Fat: 18 g
- Carbohydrates: 4 g
- Fiber: 1 g
- Sodium: 350 mg

Ingredients:
4 bone-in, skin-on chicken thighs
Juice of 1 lemon
2 cloves garlic, minced
1 teaspoon dried rosemary
1 teaspoon dried thyme
Salt and pepper to taste

Preparation:
1. Prepare the chicken thighs: Pat dry the chicken thighs and place them in a large bowl.
2. Season the chicken thighs: In a small bowl, mix lemon juice, garlic, rosemary, thyme, salt, and pepper. Toss the chicken thighs with the seasoning mixture until evenly coated.
3. Preheat the air fryer: Preheat the air fryer to 200°C (390°F) for about 5 minutes.
4. Cook the chicken thighs: Place the seasoned chicken thighs in a single layer in the air fryer basket. Cook for 20-25 minutes, flipping halfway through, until the chicken is golden brown and cooked through.
5. To serve: Serve the lemon herb chicken thighs with roasted vegetables or a salad.

RECIPES FOR AIR FRYER GARLIC PARMESAN CHICKEN BREAST

Short Description: Tender and juicy chicken breasts coated in a garlic parmesan crust, cooked to perfection in the air fryer.

Preparation Time: 10 minutes
Cooking Time: 20 minutes
Number of Servings: 4
Nutritional Information (per serving):

- Calories: 320 kcal
- Protein: 35 g
- Fat: 14 g
- Carbohydrates: 7 g
- Fiber: 2 g
- Sodium: 380 mg

Ingredients:
4 chicken breasts (boneless, skinless)
1/2 cup grated parmesan cheese
1/2 cup breadcrumbs (panko for extra crunch)
2 tablespoons olive oil
2 cloves garlic, minced
1 teaspoon dried basil
1 teaspoon dried oregano
1/2 teaspoon salt
1/4 teaspoon black pepper

Preparation:
1. Preheat the air fryer to 200°C (390°F).
2. In a small bowl, combine parmesan cheese, breadcrumbs, basil, oregano, salt, and black pepper.
3. In a separate small bowl, mix olive oil and minced garlic.
4. Brush the chicken breasts with the garlic oil mixture on both sides.
5. Coat the chicken breasts in the parmesan breadcrumb mixture, pressing gently to adhere the coating.
6. Place the chicken breasts in the air fryer basket in a single layer.
7. Cook for 18-20 minutes, flipping the chicken halfway through, until the coating is golden and the chicken reaches an internal temperature of 75°C (165°F).
8. Let the chicken rest for a few minutes before serving.
9. Serve the garlic parmesan chicken breasts with your favorite sides.

RECIPES FOR AIR FRYER LEMON PEPPER CHICKEN WINGS

Short Description: Crispy and flavorful chicken wings seasoned with lemon pepper seasoning, cooked to perfection in the air fryer.

Preparation Time: 15 minutes
Cooking Time: 20 minutes
Number of Servings: 4
Nutritional Information (per serving):

- Calories: 350 kcal
- Protein: 28 g
- Fat: 24 g
- Carbohydrates: 1 g
- Fiber: 0 g
- Sodium: 400 mg

Ingredients:
1 kg chicken wings, separated into drumettes and flats
2 tablespoons olive oil
2 tablespoons lemon pepper seasoning
1 teaspoon garlic powder
1 teaspoon onion powder
1/2 teaspoon salt

Preparation:
1. In a large bowl, toss the chicken wings with olive oil.
2. In a separate bowl, combine lemon pepper seasoning, garlic powder, onion powder, and salt.
3. Sprinkle the seasoning mixture over the chicken wings, tossing to coat evenly.
4. Preheat the air fryer to 190°C (375°F).
5. Place the seasoned chicken wings in the air fryer basket in a single layer.
6. Cook for 10 minutes, then flip the wings and cook for an additional 10 minutes, or until the chicken wings are crispy and cooked through.
7. Let the chicken wings rest for a few minutes before serving.
8. Serve the lemon pepper chicken wings with your favorite dipping sauces.

RECIPES FOR AIR FRYER ASIAN GLAZED PORK TENDERLOIN

Short Description: Juicy pork tenderloin marinated in a sweet and savory Asian glaze, air-fried to perfection.

Preparation Time: 10 minutes
Cooking Time: 25 minutes
Number of Servings: 4
Nutritional Information (per serving):

- Calories: 280 kcal
- Protein: 26 g
- Fat: 12 g
- Carbohydrates: 16 g
- Fiber: 0.5 g
- Sodium: 480 mg

Ingredients:
1 pork tenderloin (about 500g)
1/4 cup soy sauce
2 tablespoons honey
1 tablespoon rice vinegar
1 tablespoon sesame oil
2 cloves garlic, minced
1 teaspoon grated ginger
1/2 teaspoon five-spice powder
Salt and pepper to taste
Sesame seeds and sliced green onions for garnish

Preparation:
1. In a bowl, whisk together soy sauce, honey, rice vinegar, sesame oil, minced garlic, grated ginger, and five-spice powder.
2. Place the pork tenderloin in a resealable plastic bag or shallow dish and pour the marinade over it. Marinate in the refrigerator for at least 1 hour, preferably overnight.
3. Preheat the air fryer to 180°C (360°F).
4. Remove the pork tenderloin from the marinade and discard the excess marinade. Season the pork with salt and pepper.
5. Place the pork tenderloin in the air fryer basket and cook for 20-25 minutes, turning halfway through, until the internal temperature reaches 63°C (145°F).
6. Remove the pork from the air fryer and let it rest for 5 minutes before slicing.
7. Garnish with sesame seeds and sliced green onions before serving.

RECIPES FOR AIR FRYER JAMAICAN JERK CHICKEN

Short Description: Spicy and aromatic Jamaican jerk chicken, marinated with authentic Caribbean spices and cooked to perfection in the air fryer.

Preparation Time: 15 minutes
Marinating Time: 2 hours
Cooking Time: 25 minutes
Number of Servings: 4
Nutritional Information (per serving):

- Calories: 320 kcal
- Protein: 28 g
- Fat: 18 g
- Carbohydrates: 8 g
- Fiber: 1.5 g
- Sodium: 580 mg

Ingredients:
4 bone-in, skin-on chicken thighs
2 tablespoons olive oil
3 tablespoons Jamaican jerk seasoning
2 tablespoons soy sauce
2 tablespoons lime juice
2 cloves garlic, minced
1 teaspoon brown sugar,1/2 teaspoon dried thyme
1/2 teaspoon ground allspice and cinamon
Salt and pepper to taste,Lime wedges for serving

Preparation:
1. In a bowl, whisk together olive oil, Jamaican jerk seasoning, soy sauce, lime juice, minced garlic, brown sugar, dried thyme, ground allspice, and ground cinnamon.
2. Place the chicken thighs in a resealable plastic bag or shallow dish and pour the marinade over them. Marinate in the refrigerator for at least 2 hours, preferably overnight.
3. Preheat the air fryer to 200°C (400°F).
4. Remove the chicken thighs from the marinade and pat them dry with paper towels. Season with salt and pepper.
5. Place the chicken thighs in the air fryer basket, skin side down, and cook for 12 minutes.
6. Flip the chicken thighs, brush with any remaining marinade, and cook for an additional 10-12 minutes, until the chicken is cooked through and the skin is crispy.
7. Serve the Jamaican jerk chicken with lime wedges on the side. Enjoy the burst of Caribbean.

RECIPES
MAIN COURSES FISH

RECIPES FOR AIR FRYER LEMON GARLIC SALMON

Short Description: Juicy salmon fillets marinated in a tangy lemon garlic sauce, air-fried to perfection.

Preparation Time: 15 minutes
Cooking Time: 12 minutes
Number of Servings: 4
Nutritional Information (per serving):

- Calories: 280 kcal
- Protein: 24 g
- Fat: 18 g
- Carbohydrates: 2 g
- Fiber: 0.5 g
- Sodium: 400 mg

Ingredients:
4 salmon fillets
Juice of 1 lemon
2 cloves garlic, minced
2 tablespoons melted butter
Salt and pepper to taste

Preparation:
1. In a bowl, mix together lemon juice, minced garlic, melted butter, salt, and pepper.
2. Marinate salmon fillets in the mixture for 15-30 minutes.
3. Preheat the air fryer to 180°C (360°F).
4. Place marinated salmon fillets in the air fryer basket.
5. Cook for 10-12 minutes until salmon is cooked through and flakes easily with a fork.
6. Serve hot and enjoy.

RECIPES FOR AIR FRYER COCONUT-CRUSTED TILAPIA

Short Description: Crispy tilapia fillets coated in coconut flakes, air-fried to golden perfection.

Preparation Time: 10 minutes
Cooking Time: 10 minutes
Number of Servings: 4
Nutritional Information (per serving):

- Calories: 220 kcal
- Protein: 20 g
- Fat: 12 g
- Carbohydrates: 8 g
- Fiber: 2 g
- Sodium: 350 mg

Ingredients:
4 tilapia fillets
1/2 cup all-purpose flour
1 egg, beaten
1 cup shredded coconut
Salt and pepper to taste
oregano

Preparation:
1. Dredge tilapia fillets in flour, dip in beaten egg, then coat with shredded coconut.
2. Preheat the air fryer to 200°C (400°F).
3. Place coated tilapia fillets in the air fryer basket.
4. Cook for 8-10 minutes until golden brown and crispy.
5. Sprinkle oregano on top of the fish.
6. Serve hot with your favorite dipping sauce and enjoy

RECIPES FOR AIR FRYER GARLIC PARMESAN HALIBUT

Short Description: Delicate halibut fillets coated in a savory garlic parmesan crust, air-fried to perfection.

Preparation Time: 10 minutes
Cooking Time: 12 minutes
Number of Servings: 4
Nutritional Information (per serving):

- Calories: 220 kcal
- Protein: 24 g
- Fat: 12 g
- Carbohydrates: 2 g
- Fiber: 0 g
- Sodium: 400 mg

Ingredients:
4 halibut fillets
1/4 cup grated parmesan cheese
2 tablespoons olive oil
2 cloves garlic, minced
1 teaspoon dried parsley
Salt and pepper to taste
oregano

Preparation:
1. In a small bowl, combine grated parmesan cheese, olive oil, minced garlic, dried parsley, salt, and pepper.
2. Pat halibut fillets dry with paper towels and place them on a plate.
3. Brush the parmesan mixture evenly over the top of each halibut fillet.
4. Preheat the air fryer to 190°C (375°F).
5. Place the coated halibut fillets in the air fryer basket.
6. Cook for 10-12 minutes until the fish is opaque and flakes easily with a fork.
7. Sprinkle oregano on top of the fish.
8. Serve hot and garnish with additional parsley if desired. Enjoy your flavorful garlic parmesan halibut.

RECIPES FOR AIR FRYER LEMON DILL COD

Short Description: Tender cod fillets infused with zesty lemon and aromatic dill, air-fried to flaky perfection.

Preparation Time: 10 minutes
Cooking Time: 12 minutes
Number of Servings: 4
Nutritional Information (per serving):

- Calories: 200 kcal
- Protein: 24 g
- Fat: 10 g
- Carbohydrates: 2 g
- Fiber: 0 g
- Sodium: 350 mg

Ingredients:
4 cod fillets
2 tablespoons olive oil
Zest and juice of 1 lemon
2 tablespoons chopped fresh dill
Salt and pepper to taste
oregano

Preparation:
1. In a bowl, combine olive oil, lemon zest, lemon juice, chopped fresh dill, salt, and pepper.
2. Marinate cod fillets in the mixture for 15-30 minutes.
3. Preheat the air fryer to 180°C (360°F).
4. Place marinated cod fillets in the air fryer basket.
5. Cook for 10-12 minutes until the fish is opaque and flakes easily with a fork.
6. Sprinkle oregano on top of the fish.
7. Serve hot and garnish with additional dill if desired. Enjoy your flavorful lemon dill cod.

RECIPES FOR AIR FRYER COCONUT-CRUSTED HALIBUT

Short Description: Delicate halibut fillets coated in crispy coconut flakes, air-fried to golden perfection.

Preparation Time: 15 minutes
Cooking Time: 10 minutes
Number of Servings: 4
Nutritional Information (per serving):

- Calories: 250 kcal
- Protein: 20 g
- Fat: 16 g
- Carbohydrates: 6 g
- Fiber: 3 g
- Sodium: 300 mg

Ingredients:
4 halibut fillets
1/2 cup shredded coconut
1/4 cup almond flour
1 teaspoon paprika
1/2 teaspoon garlic powder
1/2 teaspoon salt
1/4 teaspoon black pepper
2 eggs, beaten

Preparation:
1. In a shallow dish, combine shredded coconut, almond flour, paprika, garlic powder, salt, and black pepper.
2. Dip halibut fillets in beaten eggs, then coat them in the coconut mixture, pressing gently to adhere.
3. Preheat the air fryer to 200°C (400°F).
4. Place coated halibut fillets in the air fryer basket.
5. Cook for 8-10 minutes until the fish is golden brown and cooked through.
6. Serve hot with your favorite dipping sauce and enjoy the crunchy coconut crust.

RECIPES FOR AIR FRYER MEDITERRANEAN HERB SEA BASS

Short Description: Flaky sea bass fillets seasoned with aromatic Mediterranean herbs and air-fried to perfection.

Preparation Time: 10 minutes
Cooking Time: 12 minutes
Number of Servings: 4
Nutritional Information (per serving):

- Calories: 180 kcal
- Protein: 22 g
- Fat: 8 g
- Carbohydrates: 2 g
- Fiber: 1 g
- Sodium: 400 mg

Ingredients:
4 sea bass fillets
2 tablespoons olive oil
2 cloves garlic, minced
1 tablespoon chopped fresh parsley
1 tablespoon chopped fresh oregano
1 tablespoon chopped fresh thyme
Juice of 1 lemon
Salt and pepper to taste

Preparation:
1. In a bowl, mix together olive oil, minced garlic, chopped fresh parsley, oregano, thyme, lemon juice, salt, and pepper.
2. Marinate sea bass fillets in the mixture for 15-30 minutes.
3. Preheat the air fryer to 190°C (375°F).
4. Place marinated sea bass fillets in the air fryer basket.
5. Cook for 10-12 minutes until the fish is opaque and flakes easily with a fork.
6. Serve hot and garnish with additional fresh herbs if desired. Enjoy your Mediterranean herb sea bass.

RECIPES FOR AIR FRYER TERIYAKI GLAZED SALMON

Short Description: Succulent salmon fillets glazed with sweet and savory teriyaki sauce, air-fried to perfection.

Preparation Time: 15 minutes
Cooking Time: 12 minutes
Number of Servings: 4
Nutritional Information (per serving):

- Calories: 280 kcal
- Protein: 24 g
- Fat: 14 g
- Carbohydrates: 12 g
- Fiber: 0.5 g
- Sodium: 600 mg

Ingredients:
4 salmon fillets
1/4 cup teriyaki sauce
2 tablespoons honey
2 tablespoons soy sauce
1 tablespoon rice vinegar
2 cloves garlic, minced
1 teaspoon grated ginger
1/2 teaspoon sesame oil
Salt and pepper to taste

Preparation:
1. In a bowl, whisk together teriyaki sauce, honey, soy sauce, rice vinegar, minced garlic, grated ginger, sesame oil, salt, and pepper.
2. Place salmon fillets in a resealable plastic bag or shallow dish and pour the marinade over them. Marinate for 30 minutes.
3. Preheat the air fryer to 180°C (360°F).
4. Remove salmon fillets from the marinade and place them in the air fryer basket.
5. Cook for 10-12 minutes until salmon is cooked through and flakes easily with a fork.
6. Serve hot and drizzle with any remaining teriyaki sauce. Enjoy your teriyaki glazed salmon.

RECIPES FOR AIR FRYER LEMON HERB TROUT

Short Description: Delicate trout fillets infused with zesty lemon and aromatic herbs, air-fried to perfection.

Preparation Time: 10 minutes
Cooking Time: 10 minutes
Number of Servings: 4
Nutritional Information (per serving):

- Calories: 200 kcal
- Protein: 22 g
- Fat: 10 g
- Carbohydrates: 2 g
- Fiber: 0.5 g
- Sodium: 300 mg

Ingredients:
4 trout fillets
Zest and juice of 1 lemon
2 tablespoons olive oil
1 tablespoon chopped fresh parsley
1 tablespoon chopped fresh dill
1 tablespoon chopped fresh chives
Salt and pepper to taste

Preparation:
1. In a bowl, combine lemon zest, lemon juice, olive oil, chopped fresh parsley, dill, chives, salt, and pepper.
2. Place trout fillets in a shallow dish and pour the marinade over them. Marinate for 15-30 minutes.
3. Preheat the air fryer to 190°C (375°F).
4. Remove trout fillets from the marinade and place them in the air fryer basket.
5. Cook for 8-10 minutes until fish is cooked through and flakes easily with a fork.
6. Serve hot and garnish with additional fresh herbs if desired. Enjoy your lemon herb trout.

RECIPES FOR AIR FRYER SPICY CAJUN CATFISH

Short Description: Flavorful catfish fillets seasoned with spicy Cajun spices, air-fried to crispy perfection.

Preparation Time: 15 minutes
Cooking Time: 12 minutes
Number of Servings: 4
Nutritional Information (per serving):

- Calories: 220 kcal
- Protein: 20 g
- Fat: 12 g
- Carbohydrates: 8 g
- Fiber: 1 g
- Sodium: 400 mg

Ingredients:
4 catfish fillets
2 tablespoons Cajun seasoning
1 tablespoon olive oil
1 teaspoon paprika
1/2 teaspoon garlic powder
1/2 teaspoon onion powder
1/4 teaspoon cayenne pepper
Salt and pepper to taste

Preparation:
1. In a bowl, mix together Cajun seasoning, olive oil, paprika, garlic powder, onion powder, cayenne pepper, salt, and pepper.
2. Rub the Cajun seasoning mixture evenly over both sides of the catfish fillets.
3. Preheat the air fryer to 200°C (400°F).
4. Place seasoned catfish fillets in the air fryer basket.
5. Cook for 10-12 minutes until the fish is golden brown and flakes easily with a fork.
6. Serve hot and enjoy your spicy Cajun catfish.

RECIPES FOR AIR FRYER GARLIC BUTTER BARRAMUNDI

Short Description: Tender barramundi fillets infused with garlic butter and air-fried to melt-in-your-mouth perfection.

Preparation Time: 10 minutes
Cooking Time: 12 minutes
Number of Servings: 4
Nutritional Information (per serving):

- Calories: 250 kcal
- Protein: 24 g
- Fat: 16 g
- Carbohydrates: 2 g
- Fiber: 0 g
- Sodium: 350 mg

Ingredients:
4 barramundi fillets
4 tablespoons unsalted butter, melted
4 cloves garlic, minced
1 tablespoon chopped fresh parsley
Salt and pepper to taste

Preparation:
1. In a bowl, mix together melted butter, minced garlic, chopped fresh parsley, salt, and pepper.
2. Place barramundi fillets in a shallow dish and pour the garlic butter mixture over them. Marinate for 15-30 minutes.
3. Preheat the air fryer to 180°C (360°F).
4. Remove barramundi fillets from the marinade and place them in the air fryer basket.
5. Cook for 10-12 minutes until the fish is opaque and flakes easily with a fork.
6. Sprinkle oregano on top of the fish.
7. Serve hot and garnish with additional chopped parsley if desired. Enjoy your garlic butter barramundi.

RECIPES
MAIN COURSES
VEGETARIAN

RECIPES FOR AIR FRYER ROASTED PUMPKIN WITH PESTO ROSSO

Short Description: Tender pumpkin pieces drizzled with olive oil and roasted with flavorful pesto rosso, creating a perfect vegetarian snack or main dish.

Preparation Time: 10 minutes
Cooking Time: 20 minutes
Number of Servings: 4
Nutritional Information (per serving):

- Calories: 180 kcal
- Protein: 3 g
- Fat: 10 g
- Carbohydrates: 20 g
- Fiber: 4 g
- Sodium: 250 mg

Ingredients:
1 small Hokkaido pumpkin, cut into chunks
2 tablespoons olive oil
4 tablespoons pesto rosso
Salt and pepper to taste
Fresh basil for garnish

Preparation:
1. Preheat the air fryer to 200°C (390°F).
2. In a bowl, toss the pumpkin chunks with olive oil, salt, and pepper.
3. Spread the pumpkin pieces evenly on the bottom of the air fryer basket.
4. Place the basket in the air fryer and roast for about 15-20 minutes until the pumpkin is tender and lightly golden.
5. Remove the basket from the air fryer and drizzle the roasted pumpkin with pesto rosso.
6. Return the basket with the pumpkin to the air fryer and continue cooking for another 5 minutes to heat the pesto.
7. Remove the roasted pumpkin from the air fryer, garnish with fresh basil, and serve as a hot snack or main dish.

RECIPES FOR AIR FRYER STUFFED BELL PEPPERS

Short Description: Colorful bell peppers filled with a savory mixture of quinoa, black beans, corn, and spices, air-fried to perfection for a wholesome vegetarian meal.

Preparation Time: 15 minutes
Cooking Time: 20 minutes
Number of Servings: 4
Nutritional Information (per serving):

- Calories: 280 kcal
- Protein: 9 g
- Fat: 7 g
- Carbohydrates: 45 g
- Fiber: 9 g
- Sodium: 480 mg

Ingredients:
4 large bell peppers, any color
1 cup cooked quinoa
1 can (15 oz) black beans, rinsed and drained
1 cup corn kernels
1 small onion, finely chopped
2 cloves garlic, minced
1 teaspoon ground cumin
1 teaspoon chili powder
Salt and pepper to taste
1/2 cup shredded cheddar cheese (optional)
Fresh cilantro for garnish

Preparation:
1. Preheat the air fryer to 180°C (360°F).
2. Cut the tops off the bell peppers and remove the seeds and membranes.
3. In a large bowl, mix together cooked quinoa, black beans, corn, chopped onion, minced garlic, ground cumin, chili powder, salt, and pepper.
4. Stuff each bell pepper with the quinoa mixture, pressing down gently to pack it in.
5. Place the stuffed bell peppers in the air fryer basket, standing upright.
6. Air-fry for about 20 minutes, or until the peppers are tender and the filling is heated through.
7. If desired, sprinkle shredded cheddar cheese over the stuffed peppers during the last 5 minutes of cooking.
8. Garnish with fresh cilantro before serving.

RECIPES FOR AIR FRYER VEGETABLE SPRING ROLLS

Short Description: Crispy and flavorful vegetable spring rolls filled with a colorful medley of vegetables, wrapped in rice paper, and air-fried to golden perfection.

Preparation Time: 20 minutes
Cooking Time: 15 minutes
Number of Servings: 4
Nutritional Information (per serving):

- Calories: 180 kcal
- Protein: 5 g
- Fat: 5 g
- Carbohydrates: 30 g
- Fiber: 5 g
- Sodium: 350 mg

Ingredients:
8 rice paper wrappers
2 cups shredded cabbage
1 large carrot, julienned,1 bell pepper, thinly sliced
1 cup bean sprouts,2 green onions, thinly sliced
2 tablespoons soy sauce,1 tablespoon sesame oil
1 teaspoon grated ginger,1 clove garlic, minced
1 tablespoon cornstarch,2 tablespoons water
Sesame seeds for garnish
Sweet chili sauce for dipping

Preparation:
1. In a large bowl, combine shredded cabbage, julienned carrot, sliced bell pepper, bean sprouts, and green onions.
2. In a small bowl, whisk together soy sauce, sesame oil, grated ginger, and minced garlic. Pour the sauce over the vegetable mixture and toss until well combined.
3. In another small bowl, mix cornstarch and water to create a slurry.
4. Dip a rice paper wrapper into warm water for a few seconds until softened. Place the wrapper on a clean surface.
5. Spoon a portion of the vegetable mixture onto the bottom third of the wrapper.
6. Fold the bottom of the wrapper over the filling, then fold in the sides, and roll up tightly.
7. Seal the edge with the cornstarch slurry. Repeat with the remaining wrappers and filling.
8. Preheat the air fryer to 180°C (360°F).Lightly spray or brush the spring rolls with oil.
9. Place the spring rolls in the air fryer basket, seam side down, in a single layer.
10. Air-fry for about 15 minutes, flipping halfway through, until the spring rolls are crispy and golden brown.

RECIPES FOR AIR FRYER VEGGIE BURGER PATTIES

Short Description: Delicious and wholesome veggie burger patties made with a blend of black beans, quinoa, vegetables, and spices, air-fried to crispy perfection for a satisfying meatless meal.

Preparation Time: 20 minutes
Cooking Time: 15 minutes
Number of Servings: 4
Nutritional Information (per serving):

- Calories: 220 kcal
- Protein: 9 g
- Fat: 6 g
- Carbohydrates: 34 g
- Fiber: 7 g
- Sodium: 380 mg

Ingredients:
1 can (15 oz) black beans, drained and rinsed
1 cup cooked quinoa,1/2 cup rolled oats
1/2 cup grated carrot
1/4 cup finely chopped onion
2 cloves garlic, minced,1 tablespoon soy sauce
1 teaspoon ground cumin
1/2 teaspoon smoked paprika
Salt and pepper to taste,2 tablespoons olive oil
Whole wheat burger buns
Lettuce, tomato slices, avocado slices, for serving

Preparation:
1. In a large mixing bowl, mash the black beans with a fork or potato masher until mostly smooth.
2. Add cooked quinoa, rolled oats, grated carrot, chopped onion, minced garlic, soy sauce, ground cumin, smoked paprika, salt, and pepper to the bowl. Mix until well combined.
3. Divide the mixture into 4 equal portions and shape each portion into a patty.
4. Preheat the air fryer to 200°C (390°F).
5. Brush both sides of each veggie burger patty with olive oil.
6. Place the patties in the air fryer basket, leaving some space between them.
7. Air-fry the patties for about 15 minutes, flipping halfway through, until crispy and golden brown on both sides.
8. Serve the veggie burger patties on whole wheat burger buns with lettuce, tomato slices, avocado slices, or your favorite toppings.

RECIPES FOR AIR FRYER STUFFED PORTOBELLO MUSHROOMS SPRINKLED WITH OREGANO

Short Description: Juicy portobello mushrooms stuffed with a savory mixture of spinach, feta cheese, and sun-dried tomatoes, air-fried to perfection for a delightful vegetarian appetizer or main dish.

Preparation Time: 15 minutes
Cooking Time: 15 minutes
Number of Servings: 4
Nutritional Information (per serving):

- Calories: 180 kcal
- Protein: 9 g
- Fat: 12 g
- Carbohydrates: 8 g
- Fiber: 3 g
- Sodium: 380 mg

Ingredients:
4 large portobello mushrooms
2 cups fresh spinach, chopped
1/2 cup crumbled feta cheese
1/4 cup chopped sun-dried tomatoes (packed in oil)
2 cloves garlic, minced
1 tablespoon olive oil
Salt and pepper to taste
Fresh parsley for garnish
oregano

Preparation:
1. Preheat the air fryer to 180°C (360°F).
2. Clean the portobello mushrooms and remove the stems.
3. In a skillet, heat olive oil over medium heat. Add minced garlic and chopped spinach, and sauté until the spinach wilts.
4. Remove the skillet from the heat and stir in crumbled feta cheese and chopped sun-dried tomatoes. Season with salt and pepper to taste.
5. Spoon the spinach mixture into the cavity of each portobello mushroom, pressing down gently to pack it in.
6. Place the stuffed mushrooms in the air fryer basket, with the stuffed side facing up.
7. Air-fry the mushrooms for about 15 minutes, or until the mushrooms are tender and the filling is heated through. Sprinkle oregano on top.

RECIPES FOR AIR FRYER VEGGIE QUESADILLAS

Short Description: Delicious vegetarian quesadillas packed with veggies, cheese, and flavorful spices, prepared in an air fryer for a quick and healthy meal for the whole family.

Preparation Time: 15 minutes
Cooking Time: 10 minutes
Number of Servings: 4
Nutritional Information (per serving):

- Calories: 280 kcal
- Protein: 10 g
- Fat: 14 g
- Carbohydrates: 30 g
- Fiber: 5 g
- Sodium: 550 mg

Ingredients:
4 wheat or corn tortillas
1 tablespoon canola oil,1 onion, thinly sliced
1 red bell pepper, sliced,1 green bell pepper, sliced
1 medium zucchini, sliced,1 cup canned corn kernels
1 cup canned black beans, drained and rinsed
1 teaspoon chili powder,1 teaspoon ground cumin
Salt and pepper to taste
1 1/2 cups shredded cheddar or yellow cheese
Fresh cilantro for garnish (optional)

Preparation:
1. Preheat the air fryer to 180°C (350°F).
2. In a large skillet over medium heat, sauté the onion, bell peppers, and zucchini in canola oil until softened.
3. Add the corn, black beans, chili powder, cumin, salt, and pepper. Cook for a few minutes, stirring, until well combined.
4. On each tortilla, spread the vegetable mixture and sprinkle shredded cheese over the top. Fold the tortilla in half to form a quesadilla.
5. Place the quesadillas in the air fryer basket, ensuring they don't overlap.
6. Air-fry for about 5 minutes on each side until crispy and the cheese is melted.
7. Remove from the air fryer and cut into wedges.
8. Serve with extra cilantro and fresh salsa on the side.

RECIPES FOR AIR FRYER CAULIFLOWER BUFFALO WINGS

Short Description: Crispy and spicy cauliflower florets coated in a tangy buffalo sauce, air-fried to perfection for a delicious vegetarian twist on classic buffalo wings.

Preparation Time: 15 minutes
Cooking Time: 20 minutes
Number of Servings: 4
Nutritional Information (per serving):

- Calories: 180 kcal
- Protein: 5 g
- Fat: 10 g
- Carbohydrates: 20 g
- Fiber: 5 g
- Sodium: 780 mg

Ingredients:
1 head cauliflower, cut into florets
1/2 cup all-purpose flour.1/2 cup water
1 teaspoon garlic powder
1 teaspoon onion powder
1/2 teaspoon paprika
Salt and pepper to taste
1/2 cup buffalo sauce
2 tablespoons melted butter or margarine
Ranch or blue cheese dressing for dipping (optional)
Celery sticks for serving

Preparation:
1. Preheat the air fryer to 200°C (400°F).
2. In a bowl, whisk together flour, water, garlic powder, onion powder, paprika, salt, and pepper until smooth.
3. Dip each cauliflower floret into the batter, coating it evenly, then shake off any excess batter.
4. Place the coated cauliflower florets in a single layer in the air fryer basket, leaving some space between them.
5. Air-fry for about 15 minutes, flipping halfway through, until the cauliflower is golden and crispy.In a separate bowl, mix buffalo sauce with melted butter or margarine.
6. Remove the cauliflower from the air fryer and toss them in the buffalo sauce mixture until evenly coated.
7. Return the cauliflower to the air fryer basket and air-fry for an additional 5 minutes to crisp up the buffalo coating.

RECIPES FOR AIR FRYER STUFFED ZUCCHINI BOATS

Short Description: Tender zucchini halves filled with a savory mixture of quinoa, vegetables, and melted cheese, air-fried to perfection for a wholesome and satisfying vegetarian meal.

Preparation Time: 20 minutes
Cooking Time: 20 minutes
Number of Servings: 4
Nutritional Information (per serving):

- Calories: 220 kcal
- Protein: 9 g
- Fat: 8 g
- Carbohydrates: 30 g
- Fiber: 6 g
- Sodium: 380 mg

Ingredients:
2 large zucchini
1 cup cooked quinoa, 1/2 cup diced tomatoes
1/2 cup diced bell peppers (any color)
1/4 cup diced red onion
1 clove garlic, minced
1 teaspoon dried oregano
1/2 teaspoon dried basil
Salt and pepper to taste
1/2 cup shredded mozzarella cheese
Fresh parsley for garnish

Preparation:
1. Preheat the air fryer to 180°C (360°F).
2. Cut the zucchini in half lengthwise, then scoop out the flesh with a spoon, leaving about 1/4-inch thick shells.
3. In a mixing bowl, combine the cooked quinoa, diced tomatoes, diced bell peppers, diced red onion, minced garlic, dried oregano, dried basil, salt, and pepper.
4. Fill each zucchini half with the quinoa mixture, pressing down gently to pack it in.
5. Place the stuffed zucchini boats in the air fryer basket.
6. Air-fry for about 15 minutes, until the zucchini is tender and the filling is heated through.
7. Sprinkle shredded mozzarella cheese over the top of each zucchini boat.
8. Air-fry for an additional 5 minutes, or until the cheese is melted and bubbly.
9. Garnish with fresh parsley before serving.

RECIPES FOR AIR FRYER VEGGIE FRITTERS WITH MARJORAM

Short Description: Crispy veggie fritters made with grated pumpkin, zucchini, and sweet corn, seasoned to perfection and air-fried for a delightful snack or side dish.

Preparation Time: 15 minutes
Cooking Time: 15 minutes
Number of Servings: 4
Nutritional Information (per serving):

- Calories: 180 kcal
- Protein: 5 g
- Fat: 8 g
- Carbohydrates: 25 g
- Fiber: 4 g
- Sodium: 380 mg

Ingredients:
1 cup grated pumpkin,1 cup grated zucchini
1/2 cup canned sweet corn
1/4 cup finely chopped red onion
1/4 cup chopped parsley
2 eggs
1/3 cup all-purpose flour
1/2 teaspoon baking powder
1/2 teaspoon salt,marjoram
1/4 teaspoon freshly ground black pepper
Canola oil spray

Preparation:
1. Preheat the air fryer to 200°C (390°F).
2. In a large bowl, combine grated pumpkin, grated zucchini, sweet corn, red onion, and parsley.
3. Add eggs, all-purpose flour, baking powder, salt, and pepper. Mix well until combined.
4. Form small patties from the vegetable mixture.
5. Spray the fritters with canola oil.
6. Place the fritters in the air fryer basket in a single layer.
7. Air-fry for about 12-15 minutes, flipping halfway through, until golden and crispy.
8. Remove from the air fryer and drain on a paper towel to remove any excess oil.
9. Serve hot, preferably with yogurt sauce or hummus for dipping.

RECIPES FOR AIR FRYER VEGETABLE TEMPURA

Short Description: Light and crispy tempura featuring a colorful assortment of vegetables, coated in a delicate batter and air-fried for a delightful vegetarian appetizer or side dish.

Preparation Time: 20 minutes
Cooking Time: 15 minutes
Number of Servings: 4
Nutritional Information (per serving):

- Calories: 160 kcal
- Protein: 3 g
- Fat: 5 g
- Carbohydrates: 25 g
- Fiber: 4 g
- Sodium: 380 mg

Ingredients:
Assorted vegetables
(broccoli florets, zucchini slices, and sweet potatoes), cut into bite
1 cup all-purpose flour
1 teaspoon baking powder
1/2 teaspoon salt
1 cup ice-cold sparkling water
marjoran
Canola oil spray
Tempura dipping sauce, for serving

Preparation:
1. Preheat the air fryer to 200°C (390°F).
2. In a large bowl, whisk together all-purpose flour, baking powder, and salt.
3. Gradually pour in the ice-cold sparkling water while whisking, until the batter is smooth and resembles pancake batter consistency.
4. Dip the assorted vegetables into the batter, coating them evenly.
5. Shake off any excess batter and place the coated vegetables in the air fryer basket in a single layer. Lightly spray the vegetables with canola oil.
6. Air-fry for about 10-15 minutes, flipping halfway through, until the temp. is golden and crispy.
7. Remove from the air fryer and drain on a wire rack or paper towel.
8. Serve hot with tempura dipping sauce on the side.

RECIPES
DESSERT DELIGHTS

RECIPES FOR AIR FRYER MINI RASPBERRY FILLED DOUGHNUTS

Short Description: Light and fluffy mini doughnuts filled with delicious raspberry filling, perfect for a sweet afternoon treat or party dessert.

Preparation Time: 30 minutes
Cooking Time: 10 minutes
Number of Servings: 12 mini doughnuts
Nutritional Information (per serving):

- Calories: 120 kcal
- Protein: 2 g
- Fat: 4 g
- Carbohydrates: 19 g
- Fiber: 2 g
- Sodium: 110 mg

Ingredients:
1 cup all-purpose flour
1 teaspoon baking powder
1/4 cup sugar,1/4 cup milk
1 egg
2 tablespoons butter, melted
1 teaspoon vanilla extract
1/2 cup raspberries, mashed
Cooking spray,Powdered sugar for dusting

Preparation:
1. In a large bowl, mix together flour, baking powder, and sugar.
2. Add milk, egg, melted butter, and vanilla extract. Stir until combined, forming a smooth batter.Gently fold mashed raspberries into the batter.Preheat the air fryer to 180°C (360°F).
3. Spray the air fryer basket with cooking spray.
4. Spoon the batter into a piping bag or a ziplock bag with a corner snipped off.
5. Pipe the batter into the air fryer basket to form small doughnut shapes.
6. Air fry for about 5-7 minutes until golden brown and cooked through.
7. Once cooked, remove the doughnuts from the air fryer and let them cool slightly.
8. In a medium saucepan, combine raspberries and sugar. Cook over low heat for about 5 minutes until raspberries break down.
9. Add dissolved cornstarch and cook for an additional minute until the sauce thickens.
10. Fill a piping bag with the raspberry filling.
11. Using a skewer or the back of a spoon, poke a hole into each doughnut and fill with
12. raspberry filling.Dust the doughnuts with powdered sugar.

RECIPES FOR AIR FRYER CHOCOLATE LAVA CAKES

Short Description: Indulge in rich and gooey chocolate lava cakes, effortlessly made in the air fryer for a decadent dessert.

Preparation Time: 20 minutes
Cooking Time: 8 minutes
Number of Servings: 4 lava cakes
Nutritional Information (per serving):

- Calories: 320 kcal
- Protein: 5 g
- Fat: 18 g
- Carbohydrates: 35 g
- Fiber: 3 g
- Sodium: 75 mg

Ingredients:

1/2 cup dark chocolate chips
1/4 cup unsalted butter
1/2 cup powdered sugar
2 large eggs
1/4 cup all-purpose flour
1 teaspoon vanilla extract
Cooking spray
Ice cream or whipped cream for serving (optional)

Preparation:

1. Preheat the air fryer to 200°C (390°F).
2. In a microwave-safe bowl, melt the dark chocolate chips and unsalted butter together in 30-second intervals, stirring until smooth.
3. Stir in the powdered sugar until well combined.
4. Add the eggs, one at a time, whisking until fully incorporated.
5. Mix in the all-purpose flour and vanilla extract until you have a smooth batter.
6. Spray four ramekins with cooking spray and divide the batter evenly among them.
7. Place the ramekins in the air fryer basket and air fry for 6-8 minutes, until the edges are set but the center is still soft.
8. Carefully remove the ramekins from the air fryer and let them cool for 1-2 minutes.
9. Run a knife around the edges to loosen the cakes, then invert onto plates.
10. Serve warm with a scoop of ice cream or a dollop of whipped cream if desired.

RECIPES FOR AIR FRYER APPLE FRITTERS

Short Description: Crispy on the outside and tender on the inside, these apple fritters are a delightful air fryer treat with a hint of cinnamon.

Preparation Time: 25 minutes
Cooking Time: 10 minutes
Number of Servings: 8 fritters
Nutritional Information (per serving):

- Calories: 150 kcal
- Protein: 3 g
- Fat: 5 g
- Carbohydrates: 24 g
- Fiber: 2 g
- Sodium: 130 mg

Ingredients:
1 cup all-purpose flour
2 tablespoons sugar
1 teaspoon baking powder
1/2 teaspoon ground cinnamon
1/4 teaspoon salt, 1/3 cup milk, 1 egg
1 teaspoon vanilla extract
1 large apple, peeled, cored, and diced
Cooking spray
Powdered sugar for dusting

Preparation:
1. In a large bowl, whisk together the flour, sugar, baking powder, ground cinnamon, and salt.
2. In another bowl, combine the milk, egg, and vanilla extract.
3. Add the wet ingredients to the dry ingredients and stir until just combined.
4. Fold in the diced apple pieces.
5. Preheat the air fryer to 180°C (360°F).
6. Spray the air fryer basket with cooking spray.
7. Drop spoonfuls of batter into the air fryer basket to form small fritters, leaving space between each.
8. Air fry for 5 minutes, then flip and continue to air fry for another 3-5 minutes until golden brown and cooked through. Remove from the air fryer and let cool slightly.
9. Dust with powdered sugar before serving.

RECIPES FOR AIR FRYER BLUEBERRY MUFFINS

Short Description: Soft and moist blueberry muffins bursting with fresh berries, made effortlessly in the air fryer for a quick and delicious treat.

Preparation Time: 15 minutes
Cooking Time: 12 minutes
Number of Servings: 6 muffins
Nutritional Information (per serving):

- Calories: 180 kcal
- Protein: 4 g
- Fat: 6 g
- Carbohydrates: 28 g
- Fiber: 2 g
- Sodium: 160 mg

Ingredients:
1 cup all-purpose flour, 1/4 cup sugar
1 teaspoon baking powder
1/4 teaspoon baking soda
1/4 teaspoon salt
1/2 cup plain yogurt
1/4 cup milk, 1 egg
2 tablespoons vegetable oil
1 teaspoon vanilla extract
1 cup fresh blueberries
Cooking spray

Preparation:
1. In a large bowl, whisk together the flour, sugar, baking powder, baking soda, and salt.
2. In another bowl, combine the yogurt, milk, egg, vegetable oil, and vanilla extract.
3. Add the wet ingredients to the dry ingredients and stir until just combined.
4. Gently fold in the fresh blueberries.
5. Preheat the air fryer to 180°C (360°F).
6. Spray silicone muffin cups with cooking spray and fill each cup about 2/3 full with the batter.
7. Place the filled muffin cups in the air fryer basket.
8. Air fry for 10-12 minutes, or until a toothpick inserted into the center of a muffin comes out clean. Remove the muffins from the air fryer and let them cool in the cups for a few minutes before transferring to a wire rack to cool completely.

RECIPES FOR AIR FRYER CINNAMON SUGAR CHURROS

Short Description: Delightfully crispy on the outside and tender on the inside, these air fryer churros are coated in cinnamon sugar and perfect for dipping in chocolate sauce.

Preparation Time: 20 minutes
Cooking Time: 10 minutes
Number of Servings: 12 churros
Nutritional Information (per serving):

- Calories: 100 kcal
- Protein: 2 g
- Fat: 4 g
- Carbohydrates: 14 g
- Fiber: 1 g
- Sodium: 75 mg

Ingredients:
1/2 cup water
2 tablespoons unsalted butter
1 tablespoon sugar,1/4 teaspoon salt
1/2 cup all-purpose flour,1 egg
1/2 teaspoon vanilla extract
Cooking spray
1/4 cup sugar
1 teaspoon ground cinnamon
Chocolate sauce for dipping (optional)

Preparation:
1. In a medium saucepan, combine the water, butter, sugar, and salt. Bring to a boil over medium heat.
2. Remove from heat and stir in the flour until a dough forms.
3. Let the dough cool slightly, then add the egg and vanilla extract, stirring until smooth and well combined.Preheat the air fryer to 190°C (375°F).
4. Transfer the dough to a piping bag fitted with a star tip.
5. Spray the air fryer basket with cooking spray.
6. Pipe the dough into 4-inch strips directly into the air fryer basket.
7. Air fry for 8-10 minutes, or until golden brown and crispy.
8. In a shallow bowl, mix together the sugar and ground cinnamon.
9. Roll the warm churros in the cinnamon sugar mixture until well coated.
10. Serve warm, with chocolate sauce for dipping if desired.

RECIPES FOR AIR FRYER PEACH HAND PIES

Short Description: Sweet and flaky peach hand pies made in the air fryer, perfect for a summer treat or a quick dessert.

Preparation Time: 20 minutes
Cooking Time: 15 minutes
Number of Servings: 8 hand pies
Nutritional Information (per serving):

- Calories: 210 kcal
- Protein: 3 g
- Fat: 10 g
- Carbohydrates: 28 g
- Fiber: 2 g
- Sodium: 190 mg

Ingredients:
2 cups fresh peaches, peeled and diced
1/4 cup sugar
1 tablespoon cornstarch
1 teaspoon lemon juice
1 teaspoon vanilla extract
1 package refrigerated pie crusts
1 egg, beaten, 1 tablespoon water
Cooking spray
Powdered sugar for dusting

Preparation:
1. In a medium bowl, combine the diced peaches, sugar, cornstarch, lemon juice, and vanilla extract. Mix well and set aside.
2. Preheat the air fryer to 180°C (360°F).
3. Roll out the refrigerated pie crusts on a lightly floured surface. Cut out circles using a 4-inch cookie cutter. Place a tablespoon of the peach filling in the center of each dough circle.
4. Fold the dough over the filling to create a half-moon shape and press the edges together with a fork to seal.
5. In a small bowl, whisk together the beaten egg and water to make an egg wash.
6. Brush the tops of the hand pies with the egg wash.
7. Spray the air fryer basket with cooking spray and place the hand pies in a single layer, leaving space between each. Air fry for 12-15 minutes, or until golden brown and crispy.
8. Remove from the air fryer and let cool slightly before dusting with powdered sugar.

RECIPES FOR AIR FRYER CHOCOLATE CHIP COOKIES

Short Description: Crispy on the edges and chewy in the center, these chocolate chip cookies are quickly baked to perfection in the air fryer.

Preparation Time: 15 minutes
Cooking Time: 8 minutes
Number of Servings: 12 cookies
Nutritional Information (per serving):

- Calories: 150 kcal
- Protein: 2 g
- Fat: 8 g
- Carbohydrates: 20 g
- Fiber: 1 g
- Sodium: 100 mg

Ingredients:

1/2 cup unsalted butter, softened
1/4 cup granulated sugar
1/4 cup brown sugar,1 egg
1 teaspoon vanilla extract
1 cup all-purpose flour
1/2 teaspoon baking soda
1/4 teaspoon salt
1/2 cup chocolate chips
Cooking spray

Preparation:

1. In a large bowl, cream together the softened butter, granulated sugar, and brown sugar until light and fluffy.
2. Add the egg and vanilla extract, and mix until well combined.
3. In another bowl, whisk together the flour, baking soda, and salt.
4. Gradually add the dry ingredients to the wet ingredients, mixing until just combined.
5. Fold in the chocolate chips.
6. Preheat the air fryer to 160°C (320°F).
7. Line the air fryer basket with parchment paper and lightly spray with cooking spray.
8. Scoop tablespoon-sized portions of dough and place them on the parchment paper, leaving space between each cookie.
9. Air fry for 6-8 minutes, or until the edges are golden brown and the centers are set.
10. Remove from the air fryer and let cool on a wire rack.

RECIPES FOR AIR FRYER LEMON BARS

Short Description: Refreshingly tart and sweet lemon bars with a buttery crust, made easily in the air fryer for a delightful dessert.

Preparation Time: 20 minutes
Cooking Time: 15 minutes
Number of Servings: 9 bars
Nutritional Information (per serving):

- Calories: 180 kcal
- Protein: 2 g
- Fat: 8 g
- Carbohydrates: 26 g
- Fiber: 1 g
- Sodium: 90 mg

Ingredients:
1 cup all-purpose flour
1/4 cup powdered sugar
1/2 cup unsalted butter, cold and cubed
3/4 cup granulated sugar
2 tablespoons all-purpose flour
1/2 teaspoon baking powder
2 large eggs
1/3 cup fresh lemon juice
1 teaspoon lemon zest
Powdered sugar for dusting

Preparation:
1. Preheat the air fryer to 170°C (340°F).
2. In a medium bowl, combine the flour and powdered sugar. Cut in the cold, cubed butter until the mixture resembles coarse crumbs.
3. Press the mixture evenly into the bottom of a greased 7-inch baking pan to form the crust.
4. Air fry the crust for 10 minutes, or until lightly golden.
5. In another bowl, whisk together the granulated sugar, flour, and baking powder.
6. Add the eggs, lemon juice, and lemon zest, and mix until well combined.
7. Pour the lemon mixture over the baked crust.
8. Air fry for an additional 15 minutes, or until the lemon filling is set and the top is lightly browned. Remove from the air fryer and let cool completely before cutting into bars.
9. Dust with powdered sugar before serving.

RECIPES FOR AIR FRYER STRAWBERRY SHORTCAKE BITES

Short Description: Delightfully light and fluffy, these air fryer strawberry shortcake bites are filled with fresh strawberries and whipped cream, perfect for a summer dessert.

Preparation Time: 25 minutes
Cooking Time: 8 minutes
Number of Servings: 12 bites
Nutritional Information (per serving):

- Calories: 130 kcal
- Protein: 2 g
- Fat: 5 g
- Carbohydrates: 19 g
- Fiber: 1 g
- Sodium: 80 mg

Ingredients:
1 cup all-purpose flour
1/4 cup sugar
1 teaspoon baking powder
1/4 teaspoon baking soda
1/4 teaspoon salt
1/4 cup cold unsalted butter, cubed
1/2 cup buttermilk
1 teaspoon vanilla extract
1 cup fresh strawberries, diced
1 cup whipped cream
Cooking spray, powder sugar

Preparation:
1. In a large bowl, whisk together the flour, sugar, baking powder, baking soda, and salt.
2. Cut in the cold butter until the mixture resembles coarse crumbs.
3. Add the buttermilk and vanilla extract, stirring until just combined.
4. Gently fold in the diced strawberries.
5. Preheat the air fryer to 180°C (360°F).
6. Spray the air fryer basket with cooking spray.
7. Drop spoonfuls of the batter into the air fryer basket to form small mounds.
8. Air fry for 6-8 minutes, or until golden brown and cooked through.
9. Remove from the air fryer and let cool slightly.
10. Slice each shortcake bite in half and fill with whipped cream.
11. Dust with powdered sugar before serving.

RECIPES FOR AIR FRYER COCONUT MACAROONS

Short Description: Crisp on the outside and chewy on the inside, these air fryer coconut macaroons are a delightful treat for coconut lovers.

Preparation Time: 15 minutes
Cooking Time: 10 minutes
Number of Servings: 16 macaroons
Nutritional Information (per serving):

- Calories: 100 kcal
- Protein: 1 g
- Fat: 6 g
- Carbohydrates: 11 g
- Fiber: 1 g
- Sodium: 30 mg

Ingredients:
2 1/2 cups sweetened shredded coconut
2/3 cup sweetened condensed milk
1 teaspoon vanilla extract
2 large egg whites
1/4 teaspoon salt
Cooking spray
Melted chocolate for drizzling (optional)

Preparation:
1. In a large bowl, combine the shredded coconut, sweetened condensed milk, and vanilla extract.
2. In another bowl, beat the egg whites and salt until stiff peaks form.
3. Gently fold the beaten egg whites into the coconut mixture until well combined.
4. Preheat the air fryer to 160°C (320°F).
5. Spray the air fryer basket with cooking spray.
6. Using a tablespoon, scoop mounds of the mixture and place them in the air fryer basket.
7. Air fry for 8-10 minutes, or until the macaroons are golden brown and set.
8. Remove from the air fryer and let cool on a wire rack.
9. Drizzle with melted chocolate if desired, and let set before serving.

RECIPES
BREAKFAST DELIGHTS

RECIPES FOR AIR FRYER CINNAMON ROLL BITES

Short Description: Soft and gooey on the inside, with a crispy cinnamon sugar coating on the outside, these cinnamon roll bites are the perfect quick breakfast treat.

Preparation Time: 10 minutes
Cooking Time: 8 minutes
Number of Servings: 4 servings
Nutritional Information (per serving):

- Calories: 250 kcal
- Protein: 3 g
- Fat: 12 g
- Carbohydrates: 32 g
- Fiber: 1 g
- Sodium: 220 mg

Ingredients:
1 can refrigerated cinnamon roll dough
Cooking spray
2 tablespoons melted butter
1/4 cup granulated sugar
1 teaspoon ground cinnamon

Preparation:
1. Preheat the air fryer to 180°C (350°F).
2. Cut the cinnamon roll dough into bite-sized pieces.
3. Spray the air fryer basket with cooking spray.
4. Place the dough pieces in the basket, ensuring they do not touch.
5. Air fry for 6-8 minutes, until golden brown.
6. In a bowl, mix sugar and cinnamon.
7. Toss the warm bites in melted butter, then in the cinnamon-sugar mixture.
8. Serve immediately for a warm, sweet treat.

RECIPES FOR AIR FRYER AVOCADO TOAST WITH POACHED EGG

Short Description: A modern breakfast classic made even easier and quicker with the air fryer. Perfectly toasted bread topped with creamy avocado and a poached egg.

Preparation Time: 5 minutes
Cooking Time: 7 minutes
Number of Servings: 2 servings
Nutritional Information (per serving):

- Calories: 350 kcal
- Protein: 12 g
- Fat: 25 g
- Carbohydrates: 20 g
- Fiber: 7 g
- Sodium: 250 mg

Ingredients:
2 slices of whole grain bread
1 ripe avocado, mashed
2 eggs
Salt and pepper to taste
Cooking spray

Preparation:
1. Preheat the air fryer to 180°C (350°F).
2. Lightly spray the bread slices with cooking spray.
3. Air fry the bread for 3-4 minutes until golden and crispy.
4. While the bread toasts, poach the eggs in the air fryer using silicone molds for 3 minutes.
5. Spread the mashed avocado on the toasted bread, season with salt and pepper.
6. Top with the poached egg, serve immediately.

RECIPES FOR AIR FRYER BANANA PANCAKES

Short Description: Fluffy banana pancakes made effortlessly in the air fryer, a great option for a healthy and delicious breakfast.

Preparation Time: 10 minutes
Cooking Time: 12minutes
Number of Servings: 4 servings
Nutritional Information (per serving):

- Calories: 200 kcal
- Protein: 5 g
- Fat: 7 g
- Carbohydrates: 30 g
- Fiber: 3 g
- Sodium: 150 mg

Ingredients:
1 cup all-purpose flour
1 tablespoon sugar
1 teaspoon baking powder
1/2 teaspoon baking soda
1/4 teaspoon salt
1 ripe banana, mashed
1 egg
1/2 cup milk
2 tablespoons melted butter
Cooking spray

Preparation:
1. Preheat the air fryer to 180°C (350°F).
2. In a large bowl, whisk together flour, sugar, baking powder, baking soda, and salt.
3. In another bowl, mix mashed banana, egg, milk, and melted butter.
4. Combine the wet ingredients with the dry ingredients until just mixed.
5. Pour pancake batter into silicone molds or ramekins.
6. Air fry for 10-12 minutes, or until the pancakes are cooked through and lightly browned.
7. Serve warm with maple syrup or fresh fruit.

RECIPES FOR AIR FRYER BREAKFAST QUESADILLA

Short Description: A crispy and cheesy breakfast quesadilla filled with scrambled eggs, cheese, and your favorite breakfast meats.

Preparation Time: 10 minutes
Cooking Time: 8 minutes
Number of Servings: 2 servings
Nutritional Information (per serving):

- Calories: 400 kcal
- Protein: 18 g
- Fat: 24 g
- Carbohydrates: 32 g
- Fiber: 2 g
- Sodium: 600 mg

Ingredients:
4 large tortillas
4 eggs, scrambled
1/2 cup shredded cheddar cheese
4 slices cooked bacon or sausage
Cooking spray

Preparation:
1. Preheat the air fryer to 180°C (350°F).
2. Lay two tortillas flat and top each with scrambled eggs, cheese, and bacon or sausage.
3. Place the remaining tortillas on top and press down lightly.
4. Spray the air fryer basket with cooking spray and place the quesadillas inside.
5. Air fry for 6-8 minutes, flipping halfway, until golden and crispy.
6. Slice into wedges and serve with salsa or guacamole.

RECIPES FOR AIR FRYER FRENCH TOAST STICKS

Short Description: Sweet, crispy French toast sticks made easily in the air fryer for a quick and fun breakfast.

Preparation Time: 10 minutes
Cooking Time: 10 minutes
Number of Servings: 4 servings
Nutritional Information (per serving):

- Calories: 280 kcal
- Protein: 7 g
- Fat: 12 g
- Carbohydrates: 32 g
- Fiber: 1 g
- Sodium: 200 mg

Ingredients:
4 slices of thick bread, cut into sticks
2 eggs
1/4 cup milk
1 teaspoon vanilla extract
1/2 teaspoon ground cinnamon
Cooking spray
Maple syrup for serving

Preparation:
1. Preheat the air fryer to 180°C (350°F).
2. In a shallow bowl, whisk together eggs, milk, vanilla, and cinnamon.
3. Dip each bread stick into the egg mixture, ensuring they are well-coated.
4. Spray the air fryer basket with cooking spray and place the sticks inside.
5. Air fry for 8-10 minutes, turning halfway, until golden brown and crispy.
6. Serve with warm maple syrup.

RECIPES FOR AIR FRYER MUFFINS WITH VEGETABLE AND CHEESE BACON

Short Description: Quick and easy egg muffins made with your choice of vegetables, cheese, and bacon, perfect for a protein-packed breakfast.

Preparation Time: 10 minutes
Cooking Time: 10 minutes
Number of Servings: 6 servings
Nutritional Information (per serving):

- Calories: 150 kcal
- Protein: 10 g
- Fat: 11 g
- Carbohydrates: 2 g
- Fiber: 0 g
- Sodium: 300 mg

Ingredients:
6 large eggs
1/2 cup shredded cheese
1/4 cup chopped bell peppers
1/4 cup cooked bacon bits
Salt and pepper to taste
Cooking spray

Preparation:
1. Preheat the air fryer to 160°C (320°F).
2. In a large bowl, whisk the eggs and season with salt and pepper.
3. Add cheese, bell peppers, and bacon to the egg mixture.
4. Spray silicone muffin molds with cooking spray and pour in the egg mixture.
5. Air fry for 8-10 minutes until the muffins are set and lightly browned.
6. Allow to cool slightly before serving.

RECIPES FOR AIR FRYER SWEET POTATO HASH

Short Description: A savory and slightly sweet breakfast hash made with crispy sweet potatoes, onions, and peppers, all cooked to perfection in the air fryer.

Preparation Time: 10 minutes
Cooking Time: 15 minutes
Number of Servings: 4 servings
Nutritional Information (per serving):

- Calories: 180 kcal
- Protein: 3 g
- Fat: 7 g
- Carbohydrates: 28 g
- Fiber: 5 g
- Sodium: 180 mg

Ingredients:
2 large sweet potatoes, peeled and diced
1 small onion, diced
1 bell pepper, diced
1 tablespoon olive oil
1 teaspoon smoked paprika
Salt and pepper to taste
Cooking spray

Preparation:
1. Preheat the air fryer to 180°C (350°F).
2. In a large bowl, toss sweet potatoes, onion, and bell pepper with olive oil, paprika, salt, and pepper.
3. Spray the air fryer basket with cooking spray and spread the mixture evenly in the basket.
4. Air fry for 12-15 minutes, shaking the basket halfway through, until the sweet potatoes are crispy and cooked through.
5. Serve hot as a side or topped with a fried egg.

RECIPES FOR AIR FRYER OATMEAL BREAKFAST BARS

Short Description: These hearty and healthy oatmeal bars are perfect for a grab-and-go breakfast, made easily in the air fryer.

Preparation Time: 10 minutes
Cooking Time: 20 minutes
Number of Servings: 8 servings
Nutritional Information (per serving):

- Calories: 220 kcal
- Protein: 5 g
- Fat: 8 g
- Carbohydrates: 32 g
- Fiber: 4 g
- Sodium: 100 mg

Ingredients:
2 cups rolled oats
1/2 cup peanut butter
1/4 cup honey
1/4 cup mashed banana
1/4 cup chopped nuts
1/2 teaspoon vanilla extract
1/2 teaspoon cinnamon
Cooking spray

Preparation:
1. Preheat the air fryer to 160°C (320°F).
2. In a large bowl, mix oats, peanut butter, honey, banana, nuts, vanilla, and cinnamon until well combined.
3. Press the mixture into a greased air fryer-safe baking dish.
4. Air fry for 18-20 minutes until the bars are set and lightly browned on top.
5. Let cool before cutting into bars and serving.

RECIPES FOR AIR FRYER BREAKFAST SAUSAGE PATTIES

Short Description: Homemade breakfast sausage patties that are juicy, flavorful, and perfectly cooked in the air fryer.

Preparation Time: 10 minutes
Cooking Time: 8 minutes
Number of Servings: 4 servings
Nutritional Information (per serving):

- Calories: 250 kcal
- Protein: 15 g
- Fat: 20 g
- Carbohydrates: 1 g
- Fiber: 0 g
- Sodium: 500 mg

Ingredients:
1 lb ground pork
1 teaspoon dried sage
1/2 teaspoon garlic powder
1/2 teaspoon onion powder
1/4 teaspoon smoked paprika
1/4 teaspoon ground black pepper
Salt to taste
Cooking spray

Preparation:
1. In a large bowl, mix together ground pork and seasonings until well combined.
2. Form the mixture into small patties.
3. Preheat the air fryer to 180°C (350°F).
4. Spray the air fryer basket with cooking spray and place the patties inside.
5. Air fry for 6-8 minutes, flipping halfway through, until fully cooked and browned.
6. Serve hot with eggs or in a breakfast sandwich.

RECIPES FOR AIR FRYER STUFFED BREAKFAST PEPPERS

Short Description: Bell peppers stuffed with a hearty mix of eggs, cheese, and sausage, then air fried to perfection for a low-carb breakfast option.

Preparation Time: 10 minutes
Cooking Time: 15 minutes
Number of Servings: 4 servings
Nutritional Information (per serving):

- Calories: 300 kcal
- Protein: 18 g
- Fat: 20 g
- Carbohydrates: 10 g
- Fiber: 2 g
- Sodium: 400 mg

Ingredients:
4 large bell peppers, tops and seeds removed
4 eggs
1/2 cup cooked sausage, crumbled
1/2 cup shredded cheese
Salt and pepper to taste
Cooking spray

Preparation:
1. Preheat the air fryer to 180°C (350°F).
2. Stuff each bell pepper with sausage and cheese.
3. Crack an egg into each pepper, seasoning with salt and pepper.
4. Spray the air fryer basket with cooking spray and place the peppers inside.
5. Air fry for 12-15 minutes until the eggs are set and the peppers are tender.
6. Serve warm, garnished with fresh herbs if desired.

SUMMARY TIPS AND CONCLUSION

Summary:

In this air fryer cookbook, you'll find a comprehensive guide to using this versatile kitchen appliance. The book is divided into key sections that cover various aspects of cooking with an air fryer. It includes essential cooking techniques, a wide range of recipes, and practical advice for both using and maintaining the appliance.

Tips:

1. Cooking Techniques: The air fryer uses hot air to cook food, allowing you to achieve a crispy texture with minimal oil. Learn how to set the appropriate temperature and cooking time for different ingredients to get the best results.
2. Recipes: Experiment with various recipes tailored for the air fryer. From classic fries to healthier versions of favorite dishes like vegetables and meats, start with basic recipes and gradually try more advanced ones.
3. Usage Tips: To achieve optimal results, remember to regularly clean your air fryer and use the right accessories, such as special mats or baking pans. Always refer to the user manual to avoid damaging the appliance.
4. Safety: Follow safety guidelines, such as not exceeding the recommended capacity of the appliance and avoiding contact with hot surfaces during use.

Conclusion:

The air fryer is a versatile appliance that can significantly simplify cooking and make it healthier. By mastering the use of hot air technology, you can prepare foods with a taste and texture similar to deep-fried dishes but with much less fat and calories. Understanding how the air fryer works, experimenting with different recipes, and adhering to usage and maintenance recommendations are key to making the most of this appliance.

With this cookbook, you now have a solid foundation for exploring all the benefits of the air fryer and enjoying delicious, healthy meals. Have fun in the kitchen and savor your tasty, nutritious creations!

TABLE OF CONTENTS

INTRODUCTION 3-4
RECIPES APPETIZERS 5
RECIPE FOR AIR-FRIED ZUCCHINI CHIPS WITH PAPRIKA FLAVOR 6
RECIPE FOR AIR-FRIED GARLIC MUSHROOMS WITH PARMESAN AND PEPPERS 7
RECIPE FOR AIR-FRIED MOZZARELLA STICKS WITH OREGANO 8
RECIPE FOR AIR FRIED AVOCADO FRIES WITH MARJORAM 9
RECIPE FOR AIR-FRIED SWEET POTATO WEDGES WITH OREGANO 10
RECIPE FOR AIR-FRIED PANKO-CRUSTED SHRIMP WITH OREGANO 11
RECIPE FOR AIR FRIED GREEK FETA BITES WITH MARJORAM 12
RECIPE FOR AIR-FRIED JALAPEÑO POPPERS WITH SAUCE 13
RECIPE FOR AIR FRIED COCONUT SHRIMP WITH OREGANO 14
RECIPE FOR FRIED ASPARAGUS WITH PARMESAN CHEESE AND MARJORAM 15
RECIPES MAIN COURSES MEAT 16
RECIPES FOR AIR-FRIED HONEY MUSTARD CHICKEN WINGS 17
RECIPES FOR AIR FRYER BBQ PORK CHOPS 18
RECIPES FOR AIR FRYER CAJUN SHRIMP 19
RECIPES FOR AIR FRYER GARLIC HERB PORK TENDERLOIN 20
RECIPES FOR AIR FRYER GREEK-STYLE LAMB CHOPS 21
RECIPES FOR AIR FRYER LEMON HERB CHICKEN THIGHS 22
RECIPES FOR AIR FRYER GARLIC PARMESAN CHICKEN BREAST 23
RECIPES FOR AIR FRYER LEMON PEPPER CHICKEN WINGS 24
RECIPES FOR AIR FRYER ASIAN GLAZED PORK TENDERLOIN 25
RECIPES FOR AIR FRYER JAMAICAN JERK CHICKEN 26
RECIPES MAIN COURSES FISH 27
RECIPES FOR AIR FRYER LEMON GARLIC SALMON 28
RECIPES FOR AIR FRYER COCONUT-CRUSTED TILAPIA 29
RECIPES FOR AIR FRYER GARLIC PARMESAN HALIBUT 30
RECIPES FOR AIR FRYER LEMON DILL COD 31
RECIPES FOR AIR FRYER COCONUT-CRUSTED HALIBUT 32
RECIPES FOR AIR FRYER MEDITERRANEAN HERB SEA BASS 33
RECIPES FOR AIR FRYER TERIYAKI GLAZED SALMON 34
RECIPES FOR AIR FRYER LEMON HERB TROUT 35
RECIPES FOR AIR FRYER SPICY CAJUN CATFISH 36

RECIPES FOR AIR FRYER GARLIC BUTTER BARRAMUNDI 37

RECIPES MAIN COURSES VEGETARIAN 38

RECIPES FOR AIR FRYER ROASTED PUMPKIN WITH PESTO ROSSO 39

RECIPES FOR AIR FRYER STUFFED BELL PEPPERS 40

RECIPES FOR AIR FRYER VEGETABLE SPRING ROLLS 41

RECIPES FOR AIR FRYER VEGGIE BURGER PATTIES 42

RECIPES FOR AIR FRYER STUFFED PORTOBELLO MUSHROOMS SPRINKLED WITH OREGANO 43

RECIPES FOR AIR FRYER VEGGIE QUESADILLAS 44

RECIPES FOR AIR FRYER CAULIFLOWER BUFFALO WINGS 45

RECIPES FOR AIR FRYER STUFFED ZUCCHINI BOATS 46

RECIPES FOR AIR FRYER VEGGIE FRITTERS WITH MARJORAM 47

RECIPES FOR AIR FRYER VEGETABLE TEMPURA 48

RECIPES DESSERT DELIGHTS 49

RECIPES FOR AIR FRYER MINI RASPBERRY FILLED DOUGHNUTS 50

RECIPES FOR AIR FRYER CHOCOLATE LAVA CAKES 51

RECIPES FOR AIR FRYER APPLE FRITTERS 52

RECIPES FOR AIR FRYER BLUEBERRY MUFFINS 53

RECIPES FOR AIR FRYER CINNAMON SUGAR CHURROS 54

RECIPES FOR AIR FRYER PEACH HAND PIES 55

RECIPES FOR AIR FRYER CHOCOLATE CHIP COOKIES 56

RECIPES FOR AIR FRYER LEMON BARS 57

RECIPES FOR AIR FRYER STRAWBERRY SHORTCAKE BITES 58

RECIPES FOR AIR FRYER COCONUT MACAROONS 59

RECIPES BREAKFAST DELIGHTS 60

RECIPES FOR AIR FRYER CINNAMON ROLL BITES 61

RECIPES FOR AIR FRYER AVOCADO TOAST WITH POACHED EGG 62

RECIPES FOR AIR FRYER BANANA PANCAKES 63

RECIPES FOR AIR FRYER BREAKFAST QUESADILLA 64

RECIPES FOR AIR FRYER FRENCH TOAST STICKS 65

RECIPES FOR AIR FRYER MUFFINS WITH VEGETABLE AND CHEESE BACON 66

RECIPES FOR AIR FRYER SWEET POTATO HASH 67

RECIPES FOR AIR FRYER OATMEAL BREAKFAST BARS 68

RECIPES FOR AIR FRYER BREAKFAST SAUSAGE PATTIES 69
RECIPES FOR AIR FRYER STUFFED BREAKFAST PEPPERS 70
SUMMARY TIPS AND CONCLUSION 71-72
TABLE OF CONTENTS 73-76

Printed in Great Britain
by Amazon